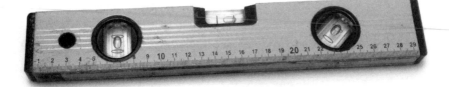

STRAIGHT TALK TO MEN
BIBLE STUDY
TIMELESS PRINCIPLES FOR LEADING YOUR FAMILY

DR. JAMES DOBSON

developed with Nic Allen

LifeWay Press®
Nashville, Tennessee

Published by LifeWay Press®
© 2014 Siggie, LLC
Reprinted 2014

Straight Talk to Men © 2014 by Dr. James Dobson. Published by Tyndale House Publishers;
Carol Stream, IL. Used by Permission.

No part of this book may be reproduced or transmitted in any form or by any means, electronic or
mechanical, including photocopying and recording, or by any information storage or retrieval system,
except as may be expressly permitted in writing by the publisher. Requests for permission should be
addressed in writing to LifeWay Press®; One LifeWay Plaza; Nashville, TN 37234-0152.

ISBN: 978-1-4300-3293-9
Item: 005650367

Dewey decimal classification: 248.842
Subject headings: MEN \ FATHERS \ CHRISTIAN LIFE

All Scripture quotations are taken from the Holman Christian Standard Bible. Copyright © 1999, 2000,
2002, 2003, 2009 by Holman Bible Publishers. Used by permission. Holman Christian Standard Bible®
and HCSB® are federally registered trademarks of Holman Bible Publishers. Cover photo: Thinkstock

To order additional copies of this resource, write to LifeWay Church Resources, Customer Service,
One LifeWay Plaza, Nashville, TN 37234-0113; fax 615.251.5933; phone 800.458.2772; order online
at *www.lifeway.com* or email *orderentry@lifeway.com;* or visit the LifeWay Christian Store serving you.

Printed in the United States of America.

Adult Ministry Publishing, LifeWay Church Resources, One LifeWay Plaza, Nashville, TN 37234-0152

Contents

About the Author

DR. JAMES DOBSON is the founder and president of Family Talk, a non-profit organization that produces his radio program, "Dr. James Dobson's Family Talk." He is the author of more than 50 books dedicated to the preservation of the family, including *The New Dare to Discipline; Love for a Lifetime; Life on the Edge; Love Must Be Tough; The New Strong-Willed Child; When God Doesn't Make Sense; Bringing Up Boys; Bringing Up Girls; Head Over Heels;* and, most recently, *Dr. Dobson's Handbook of Family Advice.*

Dr. Dobson served as an associate clinical professor of pediatrics at the University of Southern California School of Medicine for fourteen years and on the attending staff of Children's Hospital of Los Angeles for seventeen years in the divisions of Child Development and Medical Genetics. He has been active in governmental affairs and has advised three U.S. presidents on family matters.

He earned his PhD from the University of Southern California (1967) in child development and holds eighteen honorary doctoral degrees. He was inducted in 2009 into the National Radio Hall of Fame.

Dr. Dobson and his wife, Shirley, reside in Colorado Springs, Colorado. They have two grown children, Danae and Ryan, and two grandchildren.

NIC ALLEN helped with the curriculum development of this study. After spending ten years in student ministry, Nic became the family and children's pastor at Rolling Hills Community Church in Franklin, Tennessee. Nic has written for several LifeWay Bible studies, including *Courageous, Facing the Giants,* and *Flywheel.* Nic and his wife, Susan, have three children: Lillie Cate, Nora Blake, and Simon.

How to Use This Study

The four sessions of this study may be used weekly or during a weekend retreat. But we recommend that before you dig into this material, you watch the film, *Straight Talk to Men* from the *Dr. James Dobson Presents: Building a Family Legacy* film series. This will lay the groundwork for your study.

This material has been written for a small-group experience, for you and your spouse, or for personal study.

An option to extend or conclude this study is for your group to view the film *Your Legacy* from the *Dr. James Dobson Presents: Building a Family Legacy* film series.

CONNECT: The purpose of the introductory section of each session invites and motivates you to connect with the topic of the session and others in your group.

WATCH: The study DVD contains four DVD clips which include introductions from Ryan Dobson and clips from a talk by Dr. James Dobson, based on the film and the accompanying book *Straight Talk to Men* by Dr. Dobson (Tyndale Momentum; ISBN 978-1-4143-9131-1.)

ENGAGE: This section is the primary focus of each week's group time. You and the other participants will further engage the truths of Scripture and discuss accompanying questions. This section will also include a Wrap Up portion, which concludes the group session and leads to the Reflect section.

REFLECT: This at-home study section helps you dig deeper into Scripture and apply the truths you're learning. Go deeper each week by reading the suggested chapters in the book *Straight Talk to Men* and completing the activities at the end of each session in this study.

Guidelines for Groups

While you can complete this study alone, you will benefit greatly from covering the material with the interaction of a Sunday school class or small group. Here are a few ways to cultivate a valuable experience as you engage in this study.

PREPARATION: To get the most out of each group time, read through the study each week and answer the questions so you're ready to discuss the material. It will also be helpful for you and your group members to have copies of the book *Straight Talk to Men* (ISBN 978-1-4143-9131-1). Read it in advance of the study to prepare, and encourage your members to read the corresponding chapters each week. In your group, don't let one or two people shoulder the entire responsibility for conversation and participation. Everyone can pitch in and contribute.

CONFIDENTIALITY: In the study, you will be prompted to share thoughts, feelings, and personal experiences. Accept others where they are without judgment. Many of the challenges discussed will be private. These should be kept in strict confidence by the group.

RESPECT: Participants must respect each other's thoughts and opinions, providing a safe place for those insights to be shared without fear of judgment or unsolicited advice (including hints, sermons, instructions, and scriptural Band-Aids®). Take off your fix-it hat and leave it at the door, so you can just listen. If advice is requested, then it's okay to lend your opinion, seasoned with grace and offered with love.

ACCOUNTABILITY: Each week, participants will be challenged to honor the Lord and lead their families in godliness. Commit to supporting and encouraging each other during the sessions and praying for each other between meetings.

Introduction

What's right about dads?

Don't answer that. Just consider the question for a moment. The phrasing itself offers a very different perspective than the one you're most likely accustomed. You've most certainly heard many a reference to what is wrong with men in today's society. Statistics like the following provide a great deal of fodder for the already easy target.

One out of every three kids in the United States live outside of the home of their biological father. That adds up to be approximately 24 million kids.[1] These children are at least twice as likely to be poor, use drugs, be victims of abuse, and become criminals.[2] This is a widespread pandemic growing in magnitude daily. It's called fatherless children.

It's easy to see what may be wrong. Without even generalizing about the problems caused by abusive or inadequate fathers, the degree of absence among fathers does enough damage all on its own. But clear those stats and thoughts from your mind and focus on what dads do right. If your father was present when you were young, consider what he did well.

- Worked hard
- Provided financially for your family
- Taught you to respect others
- Played ball with you
- Help you apply to school
- Taught you to balance your first bank accounts
- Led you to Christ
- Modeled service in your church and in your home
- Loved your mom

Do any of these items ring true when thinking about your father? What items would make your list as a father? As you consider the items that didn't make your list, make those your goals for this study. Carefully consider the husband, father, man you'd like to be by the end.

If you're in this study, you've already taken a giant step toward being a more intentional father. It's not because this particular 4-week resource can wave a magic wand over you and your family and instantly improve the quality of your life. It has less to do with the content of this resource and more to do with the content of your heart. Being present in this study indicates a desire to grow. It's that very longing that will breed change in your life.

Jeremiah wrote the words of God in Jeremiah 29:13, "You will seek Me and find Me when you search for Me with all your heart." There will certainly be logical growth sewn into your life through the investment you make in this study. Output is always somewhat in proportion to input until you factor in the Holy Spirit. Five loaves and two fish became food for thousands. Your effort, however great, can and will yield something so much greater because of the work of God in your life as you seek Him. God doesn't hide well. It's because He so loves to be found.

If we really grasped the brevity of our lives on this earth, we would surely be motivated to invest ourselves in eternal values. Would a 50-year-old man pursue an adulterous affair if he knew how quickly he would stand before his God? Would men devote their lives to the pursuit of wealth and symbols of status if they really knew how soon their possessions would be torn from their trembling hands? It's the illusion of permanence that distorts our perception and shapes our selfish behavior. When eternal values come into view, our greatest desire is to please the Lord and influence as many for Him as possible.

Use this study to help you design your life as a father intent on blessing his children with hearts that hunger for God. Their knowledge of God and desire for God will be influenced by your knowledge and desire to a significant degree. This study is about kindling that relationship in you so that it can manifest itself in them.

If you knew your days were limited, strengthening your children's desire for God and developing better discipleship in them would be your top priorities. Remember that desire as you engage the following sessions.

WEEK 1

ON-THE-JOB
TRAINING

● **BEFORE YOU BEGIN,** pray with your group. Ask God to teach you how to be proactive, loving husbands and fathers.

Alarm.	Protein.	3 miles.
Shower.	Shave.	Gel.
Shirt.	Slacks.	Tie.
Coffee spill.	New tie.	Kiss. Hug.
English muffin.	Traffic delay.	Running late.
Meeting.	Emails.	Conference call.
Lunch across town.	Financials.	Proposal.
Traffic delay.	Running late.	Ball game.
Dinner.	Home.	Homework.
Air filter.	Sticking toilet handle.	Emails.
News.	Bed.	Repeat.

You might be tired just reading that list—even amused at just how similar it is to how you operate every day. Sure, the morning routine and basic job tasks are different. Maybe you're teaching algebra and coaching soccer, managing contractors, pulling teeth, or building sites instead of managing budgets and making proposals. It isn't the job that connects you to the time line. It's the life. And life is busy. Sometimes it's messy.

The frustrating thing about our busy lives is the perception that it's only for a season, that somehow things will slow down soon and that life will be normal again. But busy is normal. Messy is normal. The problem with busy and messy is missed opportunity. When life is so hectic, so crowded, and so repetitive, often the first thing to go is intentionality with our wives and children. Maybe you're someone who lives and breathes strategy in your career but simply goes through the motions when it's regarding family.

The point of this session is evaluation. The object is to slow down, pace your steps, and be intentional with the moments, making the most of every opportunity with your family.

What are some immediate steps you can take to be intentional regarding time with your family?

WATCH CLIP 1 from the study DVD and answer the following questions:

Are you primarily a "routine guy" or do you prefer "easy come, easy go"? Which kind of guy was your dad?

Whichever kind of guy you are, how does your routine get in the way of intentionality with your family?

How does the concept of caught vs. taught resonate with you?

What are you currently doing today to help your children know, love, and follow Christ more?

What are you not doing?

In the space provided, write down some of changes you would like to make as a dad and husband over the course of the next month. Maybe it's just a single commitment or a series of smaller goals.

CONTINUE YOUR GROUP TIME with this discussion guide.

We're introduced to many fathers in Scripture. Some are negligent and ineffective. Some are selfless and protective. One of the best examples of fatherhood, however, comes not from a biological bond, but from a discipleship-oriented one.

READ Matthew 6:25-34.

What kinds of things do you worry about?

How can seeking God correct your attitude of worry?

Jesus isn't communicating a laissez-faire attitude, asking believers to eliminate all consciousness about basic needs and provision. Like worry, idleness too is a sin. (See Prov. 19:15.)

It's the responsibility of parents, namely fathers, to provide for the well-being of their children. While worry is a sin, concern for family and hard work are godly virtues that should describe the heart of every man. Jesus isn't advocating laziness. He's encouraging us to examine our priorities and to seek a godly cure for anxiety when those priorities are out of line.

What priority can you draw from these words of Jesus?

READ Matthew 19:16-26.

According to this passage, why did the young man reject Jesus' final instruction?

What did his rejection in verse 22 indicate about his priorities?

Jesus isn't offering an additional condition to the man regarding faith. He's simply providing an indication that the man isn't as blameless as he thinks concerning the law. He loved his stuff more than he loved Christ.

> **What priorities of your own bring the most challenges in completely following Christ?**

Look at what Jesus did next. After this encounter with the rich young ruler ended, He immediately turned to His disciples with the irreducible core lesson from the experience. Jesus took the moment and made it a memory by instilling important values. He seized the divinely appointed, teachable moment to impart wisdom.

In your life as a father, those moments come when you're still, slow, and focused enough to draw out the teachable maxim.

> **Are there parts of your day-to-day schedule when you can be more intentional about communicating your values to your children? If yes, how so?**

> **Are there parts of your schedule that you can give up or slow down in order to achieve intentionality?**

● **READ** Deuteronomy 6:4-9.

> **What four moments in everyday life does this passage instruct parents to use as places to communicate truth about God?**

Look at the following list. Underline the opportunities you have as a father to teach values and communicate truth to your children that you aren't currently taking advantage of.

- When my children argue
- When my children succeed or win
- When my children fail or lose
- When natural disaster strikes somewhere in the world
- When there is conflict among adults in our extended family
- When my children are hurt or disappointed by a friend
- When my children are hurt or disappointed by me
- When my children see or hear something vulgar or provocative in the world

It's more difficult to teach proper values today than in years past because of the widespread rejection of Christian principles in our culture. In effect, there are many dissonant voices which feverishly contradict everything for which Christianity stands. The result is a generation of young people who have discarded the moral standards of the Bible.

It's possible for fathers to love and revere God while systematically losing their children. You can go to church three times a week, serve on its governing board, attend the annual picnic, pay your tithes, and make all the approved religious noises, yet somehow fail to communicate the real meaning of following Christ to your children. The greatest delusion as a father is to assume your children will be faithful Christians simply because you have been.

Now, more than ever, fathers must be intentional. You can't assume that your children are getting it. You can't assume that they recognize and accept your values. Jesus' disciples were with Him day after day and still failed to grasp so much. He maximized every opportunity to teach them. You must seize every teachable moment already available to you and be willing to let go of things and slow down. When you do this, you'll create more opportunities to teach values, instill faith, and lead your children to Christ. Nothing else matters more than this.

THIS WEEK'S INSIGHTS

• • •

- Following Jesus completely involves personal sacrifice.
- Communicating important values to your children involves equal sacrifice and focused intentionality.
- Now, more than ever, parents must seize every opportunity to communicate Christian values. And when opportunities aren't present, parents must do whatever it takes to create them.

Are there assumptions you make regarding what your children know and have learned regarding Christ and your biblical values?

What steps will you take to slow down and capture more teachable moments?

WRAP UP

• • •

PRAY TOGETHER and consider how you may seek God first as believers. Pray that you'll take full advantage of His divinely appointed opportunities to teach you children the value of seeking Him too.

Jesus, You are the Author of our faith and the
completion of it. We trust You with our lives, with
our families, with our homes, and with our decisions.
Give us the wisdom necessary to determine to do
right things and seize right moments to elevate the
value of knowing and serving You in our lives and
in the lives of our wives and children. Amen.

● **READ AND COMPLETE** the activities for this section before your next group time. For further insight, read chapters 6 and 7 from the book *Straight Talk to Men*.

THE GRIND

If you're engaging this study weekly, you've likely already won the battle to focus your attention on being a better Christian father. Perhaps you're still puzzled as to whether or not this study will prove beneficial. Maybe it took a rock bottom issue in the life of your family to cause you to desperately seek help in this way. Whatever the reason you're here, half the work is done by your willing participation.

Consider again the following statistics concerning fatherless homes:

1. One in every three kids in America (24 million) lives in a home without their biological father.[1]
2. Children from fatherless homes are more than four times as likely to be poor.[2]
3. 70% of prisoners come from fatherless homes. 80% of rapists have no dad in their home.[3]
4. Children from fatherless homes are more likely to experience teenage pregnancy.[4]

Presence is a powerful force. Spend some time reflecting on the presence or lack of presence of a father in your home growing up.

> Did you grow up with a father in your home? If yes, what roles did he play in your home? Provider? Disciplinarian? Other? Please list all.

> How would you rate the relationship you have with your father on the following continuum of closeness?

Extremely Close   No Relationship

If you were to enter the mind of your wife and answer the same question for her, how do you think she would answer regarding your relationship with your kids?

Now spend some time journaling about your context as a father and other fathers you know.

What reasons can you give for why many men have disengaged from their all-important role as a father?

What are the things that compete for your attention?

Understanding that quality and quantity are different, how do you spend quality time with your children?

SHEPHERDING YOUR CHILDREN

● **READ** John 10:11-18.

What symbol does Jesus use in this passage to describe His relationship to God's people?

How does the image of a shepherd represent fatherhood?

What does it mean for you to shepherd your family?

READ Ezekiel 34:1-6.

The priests of Israel were God's appointed shepherds for His people. The prophet Ezekiel spoke the words of God indicting the priests for abusing their role and neglecting the sheep. The easy comparison between fatherhood and this particular passage would be to all the children who are physically and emotionally abused. May God alone grant them mercy and avenge these awful crimes. But God promises to restore and do things differently in the latter part of Ezekiel 34.

READ Ezekiel 34:11-16.

How does the coming of Jesus literally and figuratively fulfill the promises of God explained in this passage?

You've likely heard that God is God of the fatherless. His constant care is for the orphan and widow. His definition of what constitutes "pure" religion is believers doing the same. (See James 1:27.) The plight of both the orphan and widow is the absence of a man to fill the role for which God created him.

READ Matthew 9:35-36.

God's love and Christ's compassion aren't what the world deserves, but what the world needs. They're what God gave to us in Christ. In the time between now and Christ's return, love, mercy and instruction are what God calls fathers to demonstrate as they shepherd their children.

VALUES = LEGACY

The world is going to forget Steve Jobs, according to a CNN article by Brandon Griggs. Hard to believe? Take it a step farther. He also writes that statues honoring Bill Gates will be erected all over the world honoring his memory. His article quotes an interview with Malcolm Gladwell, author of *The Tipping Point*. Gladwell explains that Gates' financial contributions to charities have changed people's lives—one being the funding of research to find the cure of malaria.[5] Meanwhile, Jobs' legacy of great computers and awesome techie devices, which really have revolutionized the world, was ultimately self-serving.

One could make an argument that Apple products have added extreme value to the world. One could make an equally strong argument that curing malaria would be of great value to the world. The question is which has the greatest value. It depends on what is valuable.

> **Prioritize the following items in terms of value from 1-10 with 1 having the highest value in your life and 10 having the lowest.**
>
> house   car   school   church
> career   retirement   savings   healthcare

Each of these items have value. If family, wife, or children were on this list, you would have likely prioritized them first. However, without a strong value on work, you can't provide for a family. Without adequate healthcare, transportation, or housing, it would be difficult to care for a family. Without a value on church or education, it would be challenging for you to raise children. Each of these items has value because they support a higher value, that of family.

Each of these items listed can also be used to support a very different value, that of status. The size of your home and the make of your car can help you achieve a great measure of worldly status. The salary you earn, the degree you hold, and your choices for vacation destinations are keys to growing social status in the world today.

The real value of each of the items on the list lies in the reason for it. Do you value your car because it makes you look good or because it provides safe transportation for you and your family? Do you value your home because it affords you worldly status or because it provides adequate shelter and modest comfort as you seek to make lasting memories with your family? Do you value your retirement because "he who has the most wins" or because it provides an opportunity for you to prepare for the future and bless your family as you grow older?

Values matter. What we value and why we value it matters more.

PERSONAL REFLECTION
• • •

Search me, God, and know my heart;
test me and know my concerns.
See if there is any offensive way in me;
lead me in the everlasting way.
PSALM 139:23-24

Ask God to search you and your motives and reveal false ideals and values. Although the things you deem important probably are, it's the reason you consider them so that matters. Is it self-serving or God honoring? Is it for you or for your family? Consider Steve Jobs and Bill Gates. Will your values and your reasons pad your pockets and build your fan base? Or will they change the world and build a proper legacy?

Consider your personal values. Expand on the previous list of things you prioritized. Describe also the reasons you value those things.

1. "America's Families and Living Arrangements: 2011," *U.S. Census Bureau* (online), 2011 [cited 28 May 2014]. Available from the Internet: *www.census.gov.*
2. "Fatherhood Statistics," *National Fatherhood Initiative* (online), [cited 29 May 2014]. Available from the Internet: *www.fatherhood.org/statistics-on-father-absence-download.*
3. Tony Evans, *Kingdom Man* Bible study book, (Nashville: LifeWay Press, 2012), 13.
4. "Statistics on the Father Absence Crisis in America," *National Fatherhood Initiative* (online), 2014 [cited 28 May 2014]. Available from the Internet: *www.fatherhood.org/father-absence-statistics.*
5. Griggs, Brandon. "Gladwell: In 50 years, people will forget Steve Jobs," *CNN* (online), 9 June 2012 [cited 28 May 2014]. Available from the Internet: *www.cnn.com.*

WEEK 2
BOTH/AND

● **START YOUR GROUP TIME** by discussing what participants discovered in their Reflect homework.

Do you have a favorite memory of your own childhood with your father? Describe it in the space below.

As a dad, life happens whether you're driving 75 miles an hour or sitting still in the commuter lane. You're stuck in the middle of two contradictory roles. You're called to develop your children—which takes time. You're called to provide for your children—which also takes time. There's something significant that you must understand about that time however. Time by itself isn't of any benefit to your children unless it's both meaningful and strategic.[1]

Perhaps the memory you described of your own dad was a once-in-a-lifetime experience. The family vacation to the Grand Canyon or the summer you restored your first car together. More likely, it was a simpler occurrence. The Saturdays on the lake, watching baseball, playing Uno®. The big moments you cherish wouldn't be special if they weren't the culmination of an ongoing day-to-day intentional relationship with your dad. Taking you on an annual week-long trip to Disney wouldn't have mattered if the other 51 weeks were completely void of quality or quantity time. In basketball terms, The Final Four only matters because of each regular season match-up.

As a father, you can spend every waking moment with your kids and still have little to show for the time spent. On the other hand, you can calendar one big strategic moment each year and not achieve the lasting impact you desire. It's the recipe of everyday moments mixed with significant connections along the way that compose healthy relationships.

● **WATCH CLIP 2** from the study DVD and answer the following questions:

Were you shocked by either of the following revelations presented in this clip? If so, why?

1. Kids would rather give up TV than time with dad.

2. Average dads spend less than 1 minute of quality time with kids daily.

What are the most quality moments you share with your children?

Which of your values are they learning in those moments together?

This session is about the importance of spending time with your children. How much time and what kind of time are equally important. You've already examined the necessity of imparting values along the way. This week is an opportunity to explore ways to implement and reinforce those values. Time is of the essence.

● **CONTINUE YOUR GROUP TIME** with this discussion guide.

As you discovered in the last session, you must make passing biblical values to your children a priority. And this takes time.

Children today are growing up in a wicked world. As you know, it's much deeper in moral decline than when you were born. And this world has a powerful impact on your family. Children won't be devout Christians, lovers of Christ, simply because their parents are.

If you are to ward off the wickedness that wants to devour your children, you must be present and intentional. It's the time you spend and the way you spend it that matters.

● **READ** 1 Samuel 2:12.

Wickedness isn't new. The Old Testament is full of abhorrent behavior from those who should have known and acted better. Further reading reveals specific details of how Eli's sons defiled worship practices with their self-serving desires. Looking at this story as a father, you see that the problem isn't just that Eli's sons were evil men, but that Eli knew of his sons' waywardness and did nothing to try to change it.

● **READ** 1 Samuel 2:22-25.

> According to this passage, how did Eli discover what his sons were up to?

> What does it reveal about his relationship with them?

From the outset of 1 Samuel, we encounter Eli hard at work as a priest unto the Lord. From his encounter with Hannah and Elkanah in chapter 1 to his acceptance of Samuel as a young boy in chapter 2, Eli was serious about his professional work for the Lord. His commitment to his own children, however, appeared lacking. Eli heard about his sons' behavior from townspeople, showing that his relationship with his boys was inadequate. Perhaps if had he been more involved in their lives, he would have disciplined and shepherded them—before it became too late.

Read the following verses about Samuel. Compare and contrast each with what you know of Eli's sons.

	SIMILARITIES	DIFFERENCES
1 Samuel 1:26-28		
1 Samuel 2:18-21		
1 Samuel 2:26		
1 Samuel 3:1		

Fathers can certainly not be held responsible for every decision their children make or the outcomes of their behavior. However, the responsibility fathers have is paramount and should be considered as such.

Look at the following excerpt from Dr. Tony Evans' book *Kingdom Man*:

> We live in days of constant change and motion.
> It's evident not only in technological advancement
> but also in relationships, marriages, and finances.
> With everything in motion, one of the greatest
> gifts we can give our children is stability.[2]

Do you agree with Dr. Evans' remarks on stability?

In what ways do you provide stability for your children?

In what ways do you feel the need to improve and further stabilize your family life?

You could spend a great deal of time learning about dysfunction and how to not create a stable home environment by examining the reign of Israel's most famous king, David. He had at least 19 sons and at least one daughter with multiple wives. None of this includes any children born to him by concubines and according to Scripture, there were many. (See 1 Chron. 3.) The sheer number of mouths to feed wasn't the greatest indicator of instability and dysfunction.

One example of this dysfunction comes in the story of David's two sons, Amnon and Absalom. We read in 2 Samuel that Amnon raped his half sister Tamar. This incredibly dark moment in Tamar's life resulted in the worst kind of revenge from her other brother Absalom. He killed Amnon and then eventually battled David for his throne. (See 2 Sam. 13:1-36; 15.)

READ 2 Samuel 13:37-39.

In spite of Absalom's sin and vicious rebellion, David longed to go to him, but he did not. Years passed before they encountered one another again. In all of it, David was absent. Absalom needed his father in this moment more than ever.

> Describe a time when your child really needed you
> and you were there for him or her. How did they feel?

> Now consider a moment you regret not being present
> for your child in a time of need. Have you reconciled?

Stability and security come with time. Being able to adequately disciple, discipline, and guide your children comes with credibility— the kind that is only earned through quantity and quality time.

THIS WEEK'S INSIGHTS

• • •

- You must be present in order to protect your children from the wickedness of the world.
- Relational equity fosters effective fathering. This equity is built with considerable quantity and quality time.
- Children need the stability a father can provide.

On average, how much time do you spend with your children each day?

How much daily time would you like to realistically spend with them? How will you set that in motion?

WRAP UP

• • •

PRAY TOGETHER that God would mold and shape you into fathers like He is to you. Pray you can balance your lives, prioritizing career, marriage, church, and family in a way that is honoring to Him.

Father, Your Word invokes the promise that You'll never leave us or forsake us. We trust You. We also ask You to mold us into fathers just like You, ones who are present for our children, ones who keep our promises. We rely on Your strength for the resolve to make wise choices regarding our time and the investment we make in our children. May they all live lives that honor You in part because of what we demonstrate to them. Amen.

● **READ AND COMPLETE** the activities for this section before your next group time. For further insight, read chapters 3 and 4 from the book *Straight Talk to Men*.

KIDS WILL BE KIDS

Write the names and ages of each of your children. By each, write the qualities and character traits that you love most about them, and then write the fears you have for them. Be honest with your answers.

NAME/AGE	QUALITIES	FEARS

Do you have a plan to affirm your children's qualities and to help them overcome their fears? Have you prayed about these things? Begin to think through this in the space below.

Consider the following options for a quality time with your children depending on their age:

BABIES: You likely had very little to comment in any of the questions above. Even as infants develop personalities, it's easy to run out of descriptive terms. Pick a night this week to be the one who puts them to bed. As you rock, feed, or run through their normal bedtime routine, take a moment to pray over them. Speak a promise to always be present and always be a man they can trust and depend on. Don't underestimate the power of your words, even to your infant and toddler children.

PRESCHOOL KIDS: Take them for a fun dinner with dad. Pick a place with a playground or activity that they will enjoy. During the car ride or the meal, explain to them how much you love them. Share with them the list of the wonderful qualities they possess. They'll love hearing why you love them so. As a closing activity to your night out, before bed, explain what it means to trust someone. Tell them that you have asked God to help you be a trustworthy dad. To show them what this feels like, kneel down and have them stand with their back to you two to three feet away. Extend your arms. Tell them to fall back and you will catch them. Don't underestimate the power of this trust-fall metaphor. Also, don't underestimate the amount of times they'll ask to do this again. It's an experience of trust. Each time they do it, explain that you've asked God to help you always be there to love and help them.

ELEMENTARY CHILDREN AND OLDER: Set aside some time for quality conversation. It can be over a meal or even over a weekend excursion. Go over the list of wonderful qualities you wrote on page 28 and give at least one example for each item on your list. Reaffirm your promise to always be there to help them. Ask them to trust you and explain to them that you want the absolute best for them. Offer answers to any questions they have about life, parenting, freedom, the world, or anything at all. As a showing of good faith, be really honest with them to prove your trustworthy nature and your overall desire for their greater good.

BACK TO THE FACTS

A father spends an average of 37 seconds a day with each of his children, juxtaposed with the 30 to 50 hours the average preschooler watches television each week.[3] What an incredible picture is painted by those two statistics! Do we need to ask where our kids are likely catching their values?

● **READ** Psalm 1.

> According to verse 1, why is the man happy? What about in verse 2?

It's not enough for us to avoid trouble and not lean toward the way of wicked world. Some fathers might be happy if their children end up without a public record or without an unwanted teenage pregnancy. Raising children who don't make big, earth-shattering mistakes is not a worthy goal alone. Raising children who delight in God is. Why would that ring true?

READ Exodus 20:12.

This is the very familiar parent clause found in the Ten Commandments. It's the only one with a promise that follows. Obeying one's parents leads to prosperity. Disobeying them leads to ruin.

READ Ephesians 6:1-4.

This passage explains Exodus 20:12. It reads that children are to obey their parents as they would the Lord. A careful rewording of Psalm 1:2 might be, "Instead, his delight is in his father's instruction, and he meditates on it day and night." Children don't just love time with their fathers. They love leadership from their fathers. Their desire as youngsters is to please, impress, make proud, obey, be like, and know their daddies. They want to learn from your wisdom and be taught by your side. This takes a great deal more than 37 seconds no matter how great those 37 seconds are. It's always both/and.

The Hebrew word translated as *happy* in Psalm 1 is *eh'sher* and it literally means *blessed*. And there is no greater blessing than living a long and happy life firmly inside God's promise as stated in Exodus 20:12. It comes from delighting oneself in the instruction of the Lord. His instruction is that children would obey their parents.

Do you model for your children delight in God's Word and His instruction?

Is obedience to Him evident in your life as an example to them? Discuss your thoughts below.

A PARABLE

READ Luke 15:11-32.

The point of Jesus' parable was to represent God through the forgiving father and the sons as repentant and unrepentant sinners. Consider for a moment that you don't know that this is a parable. Pretend it's just a true story. Perhaps in your life it resembles too much the story of your son or daughter.

If you were the dad in this circumstance, how would you have reacted to the prodigal's initial request?

How would you have likely reacted to his return?

Would there have been conditions on your second chance extension?

Consider your children as the elder brother. If they had a prodigal sibling, would they be jealous and object to your forgiveness or celebrate it and join the party?

Look at verse 31 again. It says that the elder son was always present with the father. Yet, we know he still didn't get it. His younger brother's sin was unrighteousness, but his was the sin of self-righteousness. It's possible for a lost sinner to be so close to the truth of God and yet never accept His grace and truth. It's possible for a child to have a godly father and never fully understand it or accept it.

If you have found yourself in a prodigal situation, don't give up. Your wayward child can return. Keep praying. Keep begging God. If your children have not left, but are fully by your side, seize every moment to make sure they truly understand and accept the truth and grace and values you live and teach. Leave nothing to chance. Make every moment count.

PERSONAL REFLECTION

• • •

How does the parable of the prodigal son relate to the relationship between you and your children?

In the space below list action steps you must take with your own schedule in order to set aside quality time with each of your children. Be specific with your answer.

1. Reggie Joiner, *Think Orange*, (Colorado Springs: David C. Cook, 2009), 68.
2. Tony Evans, *Kingdom Man* Bible study book, (Nashville: LifeWay Press, 2012), 123.
3. James C. Dobson, *What Wives Wish Their Husbands Knew About Women* (Wheaton, Ill.: Tyndale House, 1975), 157-8.

WEEK 3

VOLUME
SPEAKS
VALUE

START YOUR GROUP TIME by discussing what participants discovered in their Reflect homework.

How many times per week from August to May do you ask your children if they have completed their homework or studied for the big test? Multiple times per week no doubt. How many times per week do you instruct your children to pick up after themselves or clean their rooms? Too many to count? How many times per week, then, do you reference their daily Bible reading or personal devotion? How many times per week do you ask them how you can pray for them? How many times do you ask for their prayers by sharing your own concerns?

Volume speaks value.

Rank the following items in order of the amount of times you discuss each with your children per week.

__ Chores	__ Movies / TV shows
__ Devotions/Bible reading	__ Prayer
__ Hobbies	__ Sports
__ Homework	__ Weekend activities

READ Deuteronomy 6:5-9.

In the quest to transfer spiritual values to children, it's essential that you elevate the priority of knowing, loving, and following Jesus. If the soccer score recap supersedes conversations about Christ, you're missing the mark. The admonition in Deuteronomy 6 is to pass faith to our children. The strategy outlined includes at home when waking up and when winding down. It includes an intentional focus when en route and sharing meals.

This session is about setting and keeping priorities. It's about ensuring that your children are completely equipped. It means you must draw a clear distinction between the temporary and the eternal and train your kids to know the difference.

WATCH CLIP 3 from the study DVD and answer the following questions:

There are monumental conversations you can have with your children—including leading your child to Christ. You can also share daily moments about personal devotion, the pursuit of holiness, and worldly pressures. These values warrant greater talk time than the ball game score and even the SAT score. Knowing God, expressing amazement at His creation, and growing in Him should be a normal part of everyday conversation at home.

Have you received Jesus as your Savior and Lord of your life? If so, describe that experience.

Have each of your children reached that point in his or her spiritual journey yet?

If yes, describe the special conversations you shared leading up to that decision.

If not, list what you're doing to point them to Christ.

What, if anything, needs to take second place rather than first in your everyday conversations to make room for more intentional talk about Jesus and the pursuit of God?

CONTINUE YOUR GROUP TIME with this discussion guide.

One of the defining characteristics of fatherhood is protection. Have you seen Sherwood Pictures film, *Courageous*? It follows the lives of four fathers and their commitment to be the kind of men who lead their families well. The opening scene depicts one man hanging on for life, being drug on the side of his truck for miles, trying to stop a hijacker. When the scene ends, the audience discovers that it wasn't his truck that he was trying to save but the life of his small son who was in the back seat. Good fathers protect. They will stop at nothing to eliminate physical threats and they will also stop at nothing to eliminate spiritual ones.

READ 1 Kings 11:1-6.

> According to this passage, what directed Solomon's heart away from God?

READ James 1:13-15.

> How does this passage reflect the condition that Solomon found himself later in life?

If even the wisest man in the history of the world (see 1 Kings 3:12) can be enticed by temptation to sin by ignoring the commands of the Lord, then we need to be on guard against evil.

> In what ways have you been tempted to turn your back on God and His clearly defined path for your life?

> In what ways have you noticed temptation being an issue for your children?

● **READ** Matthew 4:4, 7, 10.

These three verses record the responses of Jesus to the temptation of Satan, which He endured during His 40-day wilderness fast.

> Note how Jesus responded to Satan's temptations.
> How might you help your kids to identify temptation?

It's not temptation itself that's the sin. It's the action and attitudes born when one gives in to temptation. Satan tempts believers to sin and to disbelieve what God has said is truth.

● **READ** Mark 9:14-27.

> Identify the key barriers that the father, the boy, and the disciples contributed to the narrative:

> In what way can you relate to the father's request in verse 24?

Consider the next spiritual steps that your children might be preparing to take. Are there particular barriers standing in their way? Barriers of unbelief, of misunderstanding, of discouragement, etc.

> How might you help them overcome those barriers?

Not only do temptation and lack of faith impede spiritual growth, false teaching does as well. Paul warned Timothy and the early church to be careful when it came to false prophets and teachers.

READ 1 Timothy 1:3-7; 2 Peter 2:1-3; and Colossians 2:8.

What do these verses claim about false doctrine?

What false doctrines or worldly "wisdom" can you name today that is competing for the hearts and minds of your children?

How can you work to eliminate false teachings from your life and the lives of your kids? Use Colossians 2:6-7 as a guide.

Until the last days, there will be an Enemy whose entire goal is to stunt the growth of the committed Christ follower. Temptation, speaking doubts about God's truth, and false teaching are all tools Satan will use, at one point or another. The goal of each Christian is to be aware of the Devil's schemes. A Christian father is to be doubly aware and should fight the Evil One on behalf of his children and must equip them to fight as they follow Jesus well.

One of the greatest threats to the institution of family today is the undermining of a father's role as protector and provider. It would be easy to draw simple conclusions about a father providing clothes for his kids and protecting them from physical harm. More difficult is understanding these responsibilities in regard to spiritual growth.

THIS WEEK'S INSIGHTS

• • •

- Major barriers to growth include temptation and lack of faith.
- Another consistent barrier is false teaching.
- The goal of Christian fathering is to provide and protect and be a catalyst for breaking down every barrier to a growing faith.

How is a father called to both protect and provide for his children spiritually?

What are two small steps you can take in order to be a better protector or provider for your kids as they continue to grow spiritually.

1.

2.

WRAP UP

• • •

PRAY TOGETHER considering how God is calling you to be more intentional fathers. Pray He will show you the areas of faith where your children need your guidance.

God, grant us all the supernatural wisdom and discernment we need to nurture the ongoing spiritual development of our children. Help us to know how to make honest assessments of who our children are. Give us insight into their walks with You, so we can know the best way to encourage their growth in You. Please, God, remove the barriers in our own lives so we can grow to be more like You, as well! We desire greater closeness and a stronger relationship with You. Amen.

● **READ AND COMPLETE** the activities for this section before your next group time. For further insight, read chapters 8 and 9 from the book *Straight Talk to Men.*

OPTIONS

Church and Culture, a website that equips the local church to confront issues within contemporary culture, posted an article in 2013 entitled "Four Families." The article explored a sociological study conducted by the Institute for Advanced Studies in Culture at the University of Virginia. The study identified four types of families. They are outlined below.

1. **THE FAITHFUL:** Composing 20% of the research population, these parents put religion at the center of their world, using morality as the supreme value and sensing that their role is to help their children determine the difference between right and wrong rooted in God's Word. 88% of these individuals are married, 74% of which are in their first marriage.

2. **THE ENGAGED PROGRESSIVES:** Comprising 21% of the research population, these parents view freedom as the supreme value and tolerance as the means to freedom's end. They want to guide their children, when faced with a morally gray area, to choose what is least offensive and best for everyone, rather than God or Scripture.

3. **THE DETACHED:** This group composing 19% is marked by a sense of uncertainty. They value "practical skills over book learning." They believe they have very little control over children or their choices. Their strategy is *not* have a strategy and let things be how they will be.

4. **AMERICAN DREAMERS:** This largest constituency composes 27%. They have low education and economic resources but big dreams for their kids. Their goal is to make life better for their children than they had it. Their highest value is on improving the future.[1]

A person can approach a study like this from many angles with very different questions.

Are there one or more categories that you find yourself caught in or between? Which ones?

Is there something about any of the categories that concerns you in regard to your friends or social circles?

READ Joshua 24:14-15.

Joshua declares to the Israelite community, now enjoying the Promised Land, that they can do what they want, how they want. He invites them to become whatever culture they desire. Yet, he announces that no matter what they choose, his family will choose to follow God.

Will your family choose God if everyone else deserts Him? Specifically how have you prepared to do so?

How is your children's faith firmly established enough that if friends, teachers, media, and culture all drift in another direction completely, they'll stand firm?

What pressures do they face as kids and what pressures do you face as a family that tempt you to move away from the above faithful 20%? Even something like year-round sports, which requires so much time, can be the very good thing that could keep your family from the best. Don't simply consider the evils of the world. Also offer up the good things that people in our culture so often place before God.

READ Deuteronomy 30:11-20.

What two options does God offer His people here, and how does this relate to the verses from Joshua 24?

● READ Matthew 7:13-14.

> How does Jesus express the two choices presented in Joshua and Deuteronomy in this section of His sermon discourse?

As a father, it's your responsibility to make the right choice, choose the right road, and then ensure that your family stays on it. It's not enough to attend church, pray before meals, abstain from certain social sins, and hope that your children glean what's necessary. It's not enough to simply hope for the best. You must actively choose to be part of the faithful and to remain faithful.

THE BATON

When a Christ-following dad is confronted with spiritual obligations and responsibilities, the Lord places in his heart an enormous burden for the spiritual wellbeing of his children. There are times when this will become so heavy we'll be tempted to ask God to remove it from our shoulders. The source of these burdens is often the awareness that a "tug of war" is being waged for the hearts and minds of our children. They'll have to choose the path they will take. And Satan would love nothing more than to deceive and destroy them, if given the opportunity.

> How have you already dealt with these burdens?

> What are specific barriers or pressures from culture that attempt to tug your children away from faithfulness?

Remember your role as a dad is to do everything you can to remove, destroy, and eliminate these barriers.

The mission of introducing one's children to Christ can be linked to a three-man relay race. First, your father runs his lap around the track, carrying the baton, which represents the gospel of Jesus Christ. At the appropriate moment, he hands the baton to you, and you begin your journey around the track. Then finally, the time will come when you must get the baton safely in the hands of your child. But as any track coach will testify, relay races are won or lost in the transfer of the baton. There is a critical moment when all can be lost by a fumble or miscalculation. The baton is rarely dropped when the runner has it firmly in his grasp. If failure is to occur, it will likely happen in the exchange between generations!

> Make a list of all the spiritual investments you are currently making (praying, daily devotions, church involvement, missional activities, and beyond).

> Now, looking at your list, in your own estimation, how well are you doing at passing the baton?

FOLLOWERSHIP

The world spends a great deal of time, energy, and resources focusing on the art of leadership. We could fill books with just the titles of other books that have been written about the subject.

Barbara Kellerman authored *Followership*, which speaks to a different side of the equation: that of the follower and the power of bottom up change. The art of following is indeed important. In fact, there is no more important concept in the world of Christianity than that of following. You follow Jesus. Your kids follow you.

● **READ** 1 Corinthians 11:1.

Remember, your children can't model what they don't find in you. The world has enough barriers that will serve as hindrances to them knowing and following Jesus. It's essential that you don't allow your misled life to be another one of those barriers. Follow Christ well with the goal that your kids will learn to do the same. Intentionally following Him is a crucial key to intentionally parenting them.

PERSONAL REFLECTION

• • •

In his book, *Follow Me*, David Platt challenges our modern interpretation of "accepting Christ in your heart" theology and introduces us to what it means to truly follow Jesus. Look the following excerpt:

> "To follow Jesus is to believe Jesus, and in order to believe Jesus, we must listen to Jesus. The life of the disciple is the life of a learner. We must constantly attune our ears to the words of our Master. As he teaches us through his Word, he transforms us in the world. As disciples of Jesus, we must be intentional about filling our minds with his truth. In the words of Paul, 'Whatever is true, whatever is noble, whatever is right, whatever is pure, whatever is lovely, whatever is admirable—if anything is excellent or praiseworthy—think about such things.' In the process of setting our minds on godly things, we guard our minds from worldly thinking. And the more we hear and know Christ through his Word, the more we will enjoy and honor Christ in the world."[2]

How should this truth impact how you influence your children?

1. James White, "Four Families," Church & Culture (online), 31 January 2013 [cited 28 May 2014]. Available from the Internet: *www.churchandculture.org*.
2. David Platt, *Follow Me*, (Carol Stream, IL: Tyndale House Publishers, 2013), 211.

WEEK 4

TOGETHER

● **START YOUR GROUP TIME** by discussing what participants discovered in their Reflect homework.

Consider for a moment the heritage that has been passed to you from your own parents and grandparents. Much of it was caught rather than taught. There were values you learned simply by being part of your family.

Evaluate the following marks of heritage and underline the qualities you learned from your parents. Then check the ones you hope to instill in your own kids, regardless of their current age or stage in life.

☐ Work hard.   ☐ Defend truth.
☐ Serve God.   ☐ Keep your promises.
☐ Love well.   ☐ Remain faithful.
☐ Stand up for justice.   ☐ Take responsibility.

Any of these things, whether you chose them all or simply checked a few, can weave together a beautiful heritage that you can pass along.

Even before they know it, children need a rich heritage. This comes from a place of love and the appropriate affection of an earthly father who loves them in a manner reflective of their Heavenly Father.

You may have grown up without the presence of a father. Or perhaps you have a father who was present physically but not emotionally. Many adult men and women were never told "I love you." Many grown men, stoic about so much in life, have melted in a therapist's chair and wept aloud because their dad never said those words.

This session is about loving your children well and instilling in them a powerful heritage rich in godly character and values, because those values are pressed into the love relationship you have with your children.

● **WATCH CLIP 4** from the study DVD and answer the following questions:

If your kids were adults today, how would they describe their heritage of faith?

Are you disconnected from your family either physically or emotionally. If yes, how?

How do you show love to your children with both words and actions? What steps can you take to make both a priority?

Love is both shown and spoken. It isn't words or actions. It's both words *and* actions. Louie Giglio writes, "God isn't honored by words alone. Like any of us, He's moved by words that are authenticated by actions."[1] You and I can identify with this. We want the words and the actions to prove them. Kids, regardless of their age, want a father who communicates an overwhelming love for them with both words and actions. A healthy legacy starts with creating an environment of love and a place where the other values, lessons, and moments can be well received and forever adhered to the fabric of their being. Love moves people. It changes us. Our children need love from their fathers.

● **CONTINUE YOUR GROUP TIME** with this discussion guide.

What would you consider the most frightening concept in Scripture? Is it God's wrath? Perhaps the nature of the world's wickedness? Perhaps the uncertainty of death or the imminence of His return?

Look at these sobering verses. Talk about frightening!

● **READ** Judges 2:9-13.

As a result of not knowing or fearing God, what did the new generation do?

As a parent, what are your greatest fears for your children? List a few below.

The greatest lurking danger waiting to attack our children is the rejection of God. Pray and be diligent to transfer a spiritual heritage to your children. This is more valuable than any monetary estate you could accumulate. Be determined to preserve a reverence and commitment to God on behalf of your children. There is no higher calling.

Remember Eli who served the Lord well as his priest? Recall what happened to his own two sons, Hophni and Phineas from session 2. Samuel was different than Eli. Surely his children faired better than Eli's, right?

● **READ** 1 Samuel 8:1-5.

What about verses 4-5 reminds you about the story of Eli and his sons?

Based on what you learned about Samuel, did you think that his children would have turned out better? Why or why not?

Like Eli's sons, Samuel's sons also dishonored God. They lived different lives than that of their priestly father. Having been part of Eli's life, one might hope that Samuel would have learned a bit more from his mentor about raising sons. Samuel, who was responsible for naming Israel's first two kings, also struggled to manage his own household.

It's humbling to consider the legacy you are building with your children and the way they will represent their father.

READ 1 Timothy 3:4-5.

Is there anything in these verses that are difficult for you to accept? If yes, explain.

Would Eli and Samuel have made the grade under these qualifications from Paul?

Describe a time when your children represented you and your heritage of faith well, making you proud.

Consider again the father-and-son-like relationship between Paul and Timothy. Paul, the mentor and leader, became a father figure for Timothy and passed an incredible legacy of faith to him.

READ 1 Timothy 6:20.

At this conclusion of the first epistle to Timothy, Paul instructs the young minister to protect the message.

What dangers faced the message about Jesus?

Your role as a father is not unlike the role that Paul pronounced to Timothy as a church leader. One of the functions of leadership in a church is to maintain sound doctrine and ensure that it's passed properly from generation to generation. As a father, your role of developing a proper heritage of faith in your children is the same. It's both a biblical mandate and an urgent command. In order for children to grow up with the knowledge of God and faith in Christ, a father must intentionally train his children. God faithfully fulfills His promise to be present and active in the lives of His people.

The greatest joy you can hope to one day receive is to watch your own adult sons and daughters passing faith onto your grandchildren.

> **List some of the most important things that you want to pass along to your children.**

> **Based on your model as their father, would it be better for your children to walk as you walk or not?**

As a Christian father, you have been entrusted with children and with the truth of God's Word. Your highest privilege and responsibility is to pass that truth on to your kids.

Enjoy your final week of personal study time. Don't consider this the end of your focus on being a Christ-centered father; this is only the beginning. The closer you are to God and His Word, the better the opportunities will be for you to invest His truth into your children.

THIS WEEK'S INSIGHTS

• • •

- The best heritage to pass on to children is one faith in God.
- Your status as a believer, even as a minister or leader, in no way guarantees the faith of your children.
- Your role as a father is to protect the truth that has been entrusted to you as you seek to pass it on fully to your children.

What parts of your life do you hope to see continue in the next generation?

What patterns of your life—perhaps things you inherited from your father—do you hope to see stop with you and not be manifested in your children?

WRAP UP

• • •

PRAY TOGETHER that God would help you protect the divinely entrusted truth and equip you to pass it to your children. Pray that you will recognize barriers from yourself and from culture that distract your children from that truth, and pray that you will rely fully on God's grace.

Holy God, You alone are Father and You alone are good. By your grace and mercy, we received this message of hope in Jesus. By your grace and mercy, faith in Christ was given to us. Help us be the men we must be in order to offer that same mercy and grace, and to instill that same heritage of faith in the children You have so generously given to us. We know Your grace and Your power. We rely fully on You. Amen.

● **READ AND COMPLETE** the activities for this section before your next group time. For further insight, read chapters 5 and 19 from the book *Straight Talk to Men.*

WHAT MATTERS MOST

You understand the concept behind beginning with the end in mind. It might be difficult to fast forward your perspective to graduation day when your child is only a toddler, but a godly father does exactly this.

Consider for a moment why keeping an end in mind matters.

● **READ** Matthew 6:19-21.

> Summarize the thesis of these three verses from Jesus' Sermon on the Mount in the space below.

Jesus says that eternal things matter much more than temporal ones.

Put it in practical terms. Tidying up one's toys has little eternal value. Being a person who takes and follows instructions from authority figures has great eternal significance. A poor spelling grade may not be cause for great concern, but a child being typecast as the lazy student will follow him forever. Being part of a soccer league as a 4th grader may be just one more activity in an already busy life. Being raised to know and understand the truth of God's Word will impact a child for life.

Every moment you spend with your children has the potential to shape them into the adult he or she will one day become. Parenting with the end in mind is essential.

● **READ** the following verses and note any specific character traits each one inserts into the life of the believer.

Philippians 4:8

Galatians 5:22-23

2 Peter 1:5-7

How do these verses contribute to your growing list of desires for your children?

The first step in developing any of those qualities in your children is to embody them yourself. In order to instill, expect, or command any of these qualities in your children, you can start by living them yourself. Being a father who practices what he preaches is a mark of integrity. A better way than commanding respect from your children is being a man worthy of respect from your children.

● **READ** Proverbs 31:26-28.

How do these verses describe a woman's worthiness?

The way her children and husband respond to her isn't staged, demanded, or required, but earned because of the qualities she possesses.

● **READ** Titus 2:2.

What does this verse say about the character of a godly man?

What do you hope and pray for your children? Consider the man or woman they will grow into to be your greatest legacy.

FOR ALL PRACTICAL PURPOSES

READ Deuteronomy 6:4-9.

What specific instructions does God give all of His people in this passage? What about to parents?

As a parent, list the top three faith principles of Christianity you hope to pass along to your children.

1.

2.

3.

This may seem like an overwhelming task. Knowing that you are to set your children's feet on the right path is clear. What is the right path?

Here's a checklist that will provide a foundation for teaching all future doctrine and faith to your children. Evaluate your child's understanding of these five concepts. As you do, place a check next to any that you find especially difficult for you.

CONCEPT 1:
"Love the Lord your God with all your heart" (Mark 12:30).

1. Is your child learning the love of God through the love, tenderness, and mercy of his/her parents?
2. Is your child learning to talk about the Lord, and to include Him in his/her thoughts and plans?
3. Is your child learning to turn to Jesus for help whenever he/she is frightened or anxious or lonely?
4. Is your child learning to read the Bible?
5. Is your child learning to pray?
6. Is your child learning the meaning of faith and trust?
7. Is your child learning the beauty of Jesus' birth and death?

CONCEPT 2:

"Love your neighbor as yourself" (Mark 12:31).

1. Is your child learning to understand and empathize with the feelings of others?
2. Is your child learning not to be selfish or demanding?
3. Is your child learning to share?
4. Is your child learning not to criticize others?
5. Is your child learning to accept himself/herself?

CONCEPT 3:

"Teach me to do Your will, for You are my God" (Ps. 143:10).

1. Is your child learning to obey his/her parents as a model for obedience to God?
2. Is your child learning to behave properly in church—God's house?
3. Is your child learning a healthy appreciation for both dimensions of God's nature: love and justice?
4. Is your child learning that there are many forms of benevolent authority outside himself/herself to which he/she must submit?
5. Is your child learning the meaning of sin and its inevitable consequences?
6. Is your child willing and able to confess their sin and receive forgiveness?

CONCEPT 4:

"Fear God and keep His commands, because this is for all humanity" (Eccl. 12:13).

1. Is your child learning to be truthful and honest?
2. Is your child learning to keep the Sabbath day holy? (How is their dad doing on this one?)
3. Is your child learning the dangers of materialism?
4. Is your child learning the blessings of living in a Christian family?
5. Is your child learning to listen to God's voice?

CONCEPT 5:

"But the fruit of the Spirit is ... self control" (Gal. 5:22-23).

1. Is your child learning to give a portion of his/her allowance to God?
2. Is your child learning to control his/her impulses?
3. Is your child learning to work and carry responsibility?
4. Is your child learning the difference between self-worth and egotistical pride?
5. Is your child learning to bow in reverence before God?

PERSONAL REFLECTION

• • •

Perhaps you're at a place of reflection looking back on mistakes you made with your children who are now older. Maybe you're not currently an active, present part of your child's life. It could be that you often find yourself busy and with little to no time to invest in your child. Maybe you're without kids, but preparing to be a parent soon. Perhaps your situation is completely unique and not summed up by any of the above. As you conclude this study, whatever situation you find yourself in, consider the legacy you're leaving. Use Ephesians 3:20-21 as encouragement.

> Now to Him who is able to do above and beyond all that we ask or think according to the power that works in us—to Him be glory in the church and in Christ Jesus to all generations, forever and ever. Amen.
> **EPHESIANS 3:20-21**

How does this passage offer you hope for the generations that follow you?

Write your own mission statement that indicates your desire to raise children that know and follow Christ.

1. Louie Giglio, *Wired,* (Sisters, OR: Multnomah Publishers, Inc., 2006), 96.

Key Insights

WEEK 1

- Following Jesus completely involves personal sacrifice.
- Communicating important values to your children involves equal sacrifice and focused intentionality.
- Now, more than ever, parents must seize every opportunity to communicate Christian values. And when opportunities aren't present, parents must do whatever it takes to create them.

WEEK 2

- You must be present in order to protect your children from the wickedness of the world.
- Relational equity fosters effective fathering. This equity is built with considerable quantity and quality time.
- Children need the stability a father can provide.

WEEK 3

- Major barriers to growth include temptation and lack of faith.
- Another consistent barrier is false teaching.
- The goal of Christian fathering is to provide and protect and be a catalyst for breaking down every barrier to a growing faith.

WEEK 4

- The best heritage to pass on to children is one faith in God.
- Your status as a believer, even as a minister or leader, in no way guarantees the faith of your children.
- Your role as a father is to protect the truth that has been entrusted to you as you seek to pass it on fully to your children.

Leader Notes

It's time for a leadership adventure. Don't worry; you don't have to have all the answers. Your role is to facilitate the group discussion, getting participants back on topic when they stray, encouraging everyone to share honestly and authentically, and guiding those who might dominate the conversation to make sure others are also getting some time to share.

As facilitator, take time to look over this entire study guide, noting the order and requirements of each session. Watch all the videos as well. Take time to read the suggested chapters (noted in the beginning of each Reflect section) from the book *Straight Talk to Men* (ISBN 978-1-4143-9131-1). And pray over the material, the prospective participants, and your time together.

You have the option of extending your group's study by showing the films *Straight Talk to Men* and *Your Legacy*. You can also keep it to four weeks by using just this study guide and DVD. The study is easy to customize for your group's needs.

Go over the How to Use This Study and the Guidelines for Groups sections with participants, making everyone aware of best practices and the steps of each session. Then dive into Week 1.

In establishing a schedule for each group meeting, consider ordering these elements for the hour of time together:

> 1. Connect—10 minutes
> 2. Watch—15 minutes
> 3. Engage—35 minutes

Be sure to allow time during each session to show the video clip. All four clips are approximately eight minutes or less in length. Reflect refers to the home study or activities done between group sessions.

Beginning with session 2, encourage some sharing regarding the previous week's Reflect home study. Usually at least one Connect question allows for this interaction. Sharing about the previous week's activities encourages participants to study on their own and be ready to share with their group during the next session.

As the study comes to a close, consider some ways to keep in touch. There may be some additional studies for which group members would like information. Some may be interested in knowing more about your church.

Occasionally, a group member may have needs that fall outside the realm of a supportive small group. If someone would be better served by the pastoral staff at your church or a professional counselor, please maintain a list of professionals to privately offer to that person, placing his/her road to recovery in the hands of a qualified pastor or counselor.

Use the space below to make notes or to identify specific page numbers and questions you would like to discuss with your small group each week based on their needs and season of life.

Further Resources

Need more guidance? Check out the following for help.

ON PARENTING:

The New Dare to Discipline by Dr. James Dobson

The New Strong-Willed Child by Dr. James Dobson

Bringing Up Boys by Dr. James Dobson

Bringing Up Girls by Dr. James Dobson

Dr. Dobson's Handbook of Family Advice by Dr. James Dobson

Raising Boys and Girls by Sissy Goff, David Thomas, and Melissa Trevathan

Love No Matter What by Brenda Garrison

Intentional Parenting by Sissy Goff, David Thomas, and Melissa Trevathan

Raising Girls by Melissa Trevathan and Sissy Goff

The Back Door to Your Teen's Heart by Melissa Trevathan

5 Love Languages by Gary Chapman

5 Conversations You Must Have with Your Daughter by Vicki Courtney

Parenting Teens magazine

HomeLife magazine

ParentLife magazine

The Parent Adventure by Selma and Rodney Wilson

Experiencing God at Home by Richard Blackaby and Tom Blackaby

Love Dare for Parents by Stephen Kendrick and Alex Kendrick

Authentic Parenting in a Postmodern Culture by Mary E. DeMuth

Grace-Based Parenting by Tim Kimmel

ON DISCUSSING FAITH WITH YOUR CHILDREN:

Bringing the Gospel Home by Randy Newman

Firsthand by Ryan Shook and Josh Shook

God Distorted by John Bishop

Sticky Faith by Dr. Kara E. Powell and Dr. Chap Clark

Parenting Beyond Your Capacity by Reggie Joiner and Carey Nieuwhof

A Praying Life by Paul Miller

Faith Conversations for Families by Jim Burns

Introducing Your Child to Christ

Your most significant calling and privilege as a parent is to introduce your children to Jesus Christ. A good way to begin this conversation is to tell them about your own faith journey.

Outlined below is a simple gospel presentation you can share with your child. Define any terms they don't understand and make it more conversational, letting the Spirit guide your words and allowing your child to ask questions and contribute along the way.

GOD RULES. The Bible tells us God created everything, and He's in charge of everything. (See Gen. 1:1; Col. 1:16-17; Rev. 4:11.)

WE SINNED. We all choose to disobey God. The Bible calls this sin. Sin separates us from God and deserves God's punishment of death. (See Rom. 3:23; 6:23.)

GOD PROVIDED. God sent Jesus, the perfect solution to our sin problem, to rescue us from the punishment we deserve. It's something we, as sinners, could never earn on our own. Jesus alone saves us. (See John 3:16; Eph. 2:8-9.)

JESUS GIVES. He lived a perfect life, died on the cross for our sins, and rose again. Because Jesus gave up His life for us, we can be welcomed into God's family for eternity. This is the best gift ever! (See Rom. 5:8; 2 Cor. 5:21; Eph. 2:8-9; 1 Pet. 3:18.)

WE RESPOND. Believe in your heart that Jesus alone saves you through what He's already done on the cross. Repent, by turning away from your sin. Tell God and others that your faith is in Jesus. (See John 14:6; Rom. 10:9-10,13.)

If your child is ready to respond, explain what it means for Jesus to be Lord of his or her life. Guide your child to a time in prayer to repent and express his or her belief in Jesus. If your child responds in faith, celebrate! You now have the opportunity to disciple your child to be more like Christ.

BUILD YOUR FAMILY LEGACY.

Dr. James Dobson leads you through his classic messages and new insights for today's families in these eight DVD-based Bible studies. Each Building a Family Legacy Bible study includes four-sessions with personal reflection and discussion guides along with a DVD of Dr. Dobson's teachings, introduced by his son, Ryan. Studies include:

Your Legacy Bible Study
Bringing Up Boys Bible Study
Bringing Up Girls Bible Study
Dare to Discipline Bible Study
The Strong-Willed Child Bible Study
Straight Talk to Men Bible Study
Love for a Lifetime Bible Study
Wanting to Believe Bible Study

Learn more at LifeWay.com/Legacy

DR. JAMES DOBSON BUILDING A FAMILY LEGACY™

Dr. James Dobson's **BUILDING A FAMILY LEGACY** campaign includes films, Bible studies, and books designed to help families of all ages and stages. Dr. Dobson's wisdom, insight, and humor promise to strengthen marriages and help parents meet the remarkable challenges of raising children. Most importantly, **BUILDING A FAMILY LEGACY** will inspire parents to lead their children to personal faith in Jesus Christ.

Learn more at

BUILDINGAFAMILYLEGACY.COM

BUILDING A FAMILY LEGACY BOOKS

From Dr. James Dobson and Tyndale Momentum

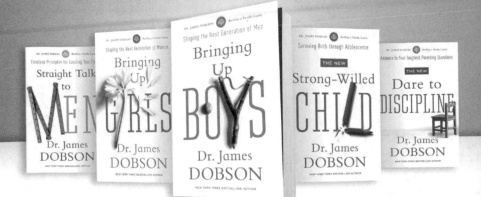

Bringing Up Boys • 978-1-4143-9133-5
Also available in hardcover (978-0-8423-5266-6) and audio CDs
(978-0-8423-2297-3)

Bringing Up Girls • 978-1-4143-9132-8
Also available in hardcover (978-1-4143-0127-3) and audio CDs
read by Dr. James Dobson (978-1-4143-3650-3)

The New Strong-Willed Child • 978-1-4143-9134-2
Also available in hardcover (978-0-8423-3622-2) and audio
CDs (978-0-8423-8799-6), as well as *The New Strong-Willed
Child Workbook* (978-1-4143-0382-6)

The New Dare to Discipline • 978-1-4143-9135-9

Straight Talk to Men • 978-1-4143-9131-1

AVAILABLE IN 2015

Love for a Lifetime
Revised and expanded edition
978-1-4964-0328-5